Universe & You

11 Steps To Co-Create The Life You Desire

Universe & You

11 Steps To Co-Create The Life You Desire

Lais Stephan
www.laisstephan.com

The author of this book does not dispense medical advice
or prescribe the use of any technique as a form for
physical, emotional, or medical problems without the
advice of a physical, either directly or indirectly. The
intent of the author is only to offer information of a
general nature to help you in your quest for emotional
and spiritual well-being. In the event you use any of the
information, the meditations or any of the exercises in
this book for yourself, the author assumes no
responsibility for your actions.

ISBN: 978-2-9701480-0-5
Book design and illustrations by Ces Rosanna Price
Visit www.laisstephan.com

Isa, my little Earth angel, I dedicate this book to you. I'm so blessed to have grown up with you. Thank you for continuously teaching me the magic of unconditional love. Without you this book wouldn't exist.

Table of Contents

Introduction

Dear Reader,

I am more than thrilled to have you read this book and trust me when I say that the Universe can't wait to connect with you soon. Most chapters in this book will be written in the Universe's point of view and it's the Universe who will explain what this "co-creation business" is all about and how you get to increase your co-creation energy in order to create the life you desire to live.

I am smiling while writing this because "Universe & You" is the result of my most favourite relationship of all: my relationship with the Universe. This introduction is the story of how it all began.

I was born in South Brazil but grew up in a small picturesque town in Germany. You might have heard of the Pied Piper of Hamelin legend – that's where I'm from. Growing up, I wanted to besuccessful like my father, who was running a global company and who took me along on some international business trips to Singapore and the US.

When I was just out of university with a Business & Italian Honours degree, I was ready to take the corporate world by storm. After some initial work experience in the UK, I was soon hired by one of the biggest Fast Moving Consumer Good companies in the world at their European headquarters in Geneva, Switzerland. I had even been assigned to one of their most profitable departments: detergents. I would be earning some decent money and could start to build my empire. Eight months later, I was fired. Oops! What happened?

The very first day I stepped into the open-space office, my stomach churned and knotted itself into a double fisherman's knot. I knew I didn't belong there. I was responsible for things like understanding whether detergent bottles should be red or blue and how much scent consumers wanted. To say I was bored would be an understatement, so I channelled all my enthusiasm into spending my days having coffees on different floors of the building with fellow expat colleagues and by night, excelling as a party organiser.

When I was asked to accompany the director of the department and my manager into a small huddle room with glass windows, my heart sank into my boots. They didn't waste much time telling me they would have to let me go. I was both shocked and relieved at the same time.

"Geez, what took you so long?" I almost asked them. Then I realised I wasn't entitled to unemployment benefits because I hadn't lived in Switzerland for a full year and I only had two–three months' worth of savings.

At that point, I had just started to date a man who was working for the foreign ministry of Azerbaijan, a country I had difficulty finding on a map. When his mission in Geneva ended, I decided I wouldn't wait to get fired from my corporate job again and that working for NGOs in Azerbaijan would be a better use of my time.

I followed him to Baku and worked for different NGOs. But guess what: it turns out that following someone you just started dating to a different country isn't a great idea. Working for NGOs wasn't as rewarding and fulfilling as I had hoped either. After six months, I fled that karmic relationship like it was the running of the bulls in Pamplona and landed back in Europe. I broke down on my bathroom floor, barely able to move. I was burned out: emotionally, mentally and physically. I had also been constantly suffering from bronchitis and migraines, which kept me low on energy.

Being 30 years old, single, unemployed and suffering from a low immune system wasn't exactly my idea of a happy and fulfilled life. I felt like an ugly worm and even worse: an ugly worm without a life purpose. How had life even gotten to this point? Where was my sliding doors moment – that crucial moment when I could have made a different decision and life would have turned out very differently?

Then I did the only thing I hadn't tried yet: pray.

"Hello, anybody up there? I think I might have hit rock bottom. Any tips on how to get myself out of this mess?" I sobbed.

"Heal yourself." The answer came right away. I felt an external energy with me and an enormous amount of love and compassion.

"Heal myself?" I wondered. Even though I didn't know yet what that would look like, the thought of it was comforting.

I thought about how I had suffered from a debilitating depression as a teenager and how growing up in a dysfunctional family with a depressed, alcoholic father and a co-dependent mother made me run away from home. I thought about how not long after I fell apart, I was admitted into a clinic specialising in depression, where I stayed, heavily medicated, for many weeks. I knew I didn't want to go down that route again and that this time around, my healing needed to look different.

I spent a few days researching and came up with a master plan: I would fly to Thailand to study different energy healing methods, meditation and practice yoga for a month.

"Bye, I am off to Thailand to become the queen of balanced chakras!" I told everyone without knowing what chakras actually were.

And so I was introduced to the fascinating world of self-healing, where I learned how to channel high-level energy to balance my energy system (aka my chakras) and how to visualise and communicate with the Universe as well as my spirit guides. Even my Brazilian grandma Rosa, who had died the year before, was with me in Thailand during my transformation. Other energy healers would see her when they gave me a session and ask, "Who is that fashionable elderly spirit lady?"

I spent some time healing from my karmic relationship because in order to find a more stable and healthy relationship, I needed to heal from my relationship, or rather non-relationship, with my father. Otherwise, I would always attract men who were as emotionally available as a wax figure at Madame Tussauds.

Being able to communicate with my "invisible helpers", as I lovingly call them, was one of the most rewarding and healing components of my self-development journey. I understood that it was the Universe who had been with me on that bathroom floor and had guided me during my entire healing journey.

Of course, I had far more to heal than the end of a toxic relationship and my inability to feel fulfilled in a corporate job or any conventional office job. These things were just the tip of the iceberg. The month I had planned to stay in Thailand stretched into an entire year. I came with heavy ancestral baggage, past life traumas, sad womb memories, and endless limiting beliefs and fears, as well as repressed emotions, which were lowering my energy and thus my ability to co-create a better life for myself.

While I was healing from all of the above, I also had to practice what I was learning on others in order to get certified as an energy therapist. It's difficult to describe the joy I felt when I was part of someone else's healing journey. Due to my healing, I was able to reconnect to my until-then dormant intuitive gifts and started to receive messages for the people I was healing: be it past life visions, messages from their spirit guides or root causes for their suffering. I had never felt that level of fulfilment before and it dawned on me that my life purpose looked very different than I had expected. I had been looking for success and money in the wrong places because I had desperately tried to be like my father so he would be proud of me.

Since then, the Universe and I have come a long way. It has always guided me, taught me, and communicated with me, sending me signs, love, and healing when I needed it. But once I learned how to visualise and channel messages from the Universe, that's when our conversations started. That's also how I learned that the Universe is full of humour.

It taught me there is more to co-creation than just the "ask and it is given" advice many law of attraction mentors teach. There is more that can be done than just creating vision boards and repeating affirmations.

These things have their place in the co-creation journey – of course they do – but on their own, they are not enough. Especially not when someone, like me, comes with heavy baggage that needs to be released first, otherwise one keeps repeating negative patterns in many different ways and forms.

We need to have at least 11 things in place when we consistently wish to co-create an upleveling in our lives.

Ever since I embarked on my co-creation journey towards upleveling my life, I have:

☆ Created a healing business which worked from the first month and which is location-independent, allowing me to travel and live in amazing different places.

☆ Found a man who is emotionally available, caring, and loving, who isn't afraid of my success or power, and who keeps me grounded.

☆ Said good-bye to relationships with people who were draining my energy and developed strong and healthy boundaries.

☆ Said good-bye to bronchitis and migraines. I haven't had the flu for more than a decade, nor any other illness.

☆ Have co-created a life filled with purpose, inspiration, and creativity that allows me to be a multi-passionate, creative woman with enough time to explore my many other hobbies, such as writing, painting, and poetry.

Of course, my co-creation journey didn't happen overnight. It's the result of consistently practicing the 11 steps outlined in this book. Co-creation is like a muscle we need to build up and which disappears if we stop. Our relationship with the Universe is like any other relationship: the more time and energy we put into it and nurture it, the better it becomes.

I have been working with women for a decade now, helping them release energetic blockages caused by past traumas and teaching them how to empower themselves to create the life they desire and deserve.

We all have the capacity to create better lives for ourselves. We are all deserving of healthier, more loving and respectful relationships, advancing our careers, running a successful business, or being emotionally, mentally and physically healthy, as well as having the right tools to cope with the challenges life consistently throws at us.

This book comes with 12 powerful meditations. You can listen to them via the link below:

https://bit.ly/3afPLCM

How This Book Works

Whatever it is you desire to be, become or have, and whatever area you wish to uplevel in your life, the 11-step process in this book will help you get there.

This book is for you if you wish to:

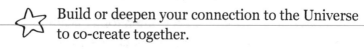 Build or deepen your connection to the Universe to co-create together.

⭐ Build or deepen your intuitive abilities (which we all have).

⭐ Release energetic blockages from your past, preventing you from upleveling your life.

⭐ Invite in more gratitude and self-compassion.

⭐ Learn how to become truly magnetic for the things you desire to achieve, have or be.

⭐ Help the collective field of all women to co-create their desires.

How To Work Through The Chapters

Your co-creation journey will work best if you work through the chapters and accompanying meditations regularly and consistently without letting too much time pass between chapters. Once you start building up your co-creation energy, it's in your highest interest to keep it flowing. Create a little ritual, be it a daily or weekly routine, to work through the short chapters. Make sure you have a dedicated journal next to you once you finish a meditation. You never know what kind of nuggets of wisdom you might receive.

The Universe Will Be With You

From the minute you start working through this book, the Universe, or whatever you call that Higher Power for yourself, will be by your side. It will be deeply involved in your co-creation journey and the healing that needs to take place to get you closer to your goal. For some of you, it might be a smooth and easy ride, for others it might bring up some old repressed emotions. Whatever arises and wishes to be expressed is absolutely divine. Make space for your emotional landscape to present itself to you fully: let the tears flow or old anger knock on your door. Make time to witness what is arising within you with curiosity and non-judgment before you release it. It's not having "negative" emotions that lower our energetic frequency, but the judgment of having them. See this journey as a self-compassionate one: If you get only one thing out of this book, I really hope it'll be more self-compassion.

Get Ready To Co-Create For The Collective Field Of All Women

By working on yourself, you will be helping the collective field of all women, cis gender and transgender alike. As women, we have to work harder to be seen, acknowledged and taken seriously. We have to prove ourselves more. We may have experienced sexual harassment or worse, or at the very least, know several women who have.

I don't believe that we can change structural and institutional sexism and/or racism just by doing a few visualisations and meditations here and there. Far from it.

We can't advance until all women can advance. If we are co-creating something important for ourselves, let's include all women as part of that journey. Our intentions are powerful: the more we co-create selflessly, and focus on co-creating for the collective field of all women, the quicker we can advance. What starts with an intention will ultimately motivate you to also take action and support women in your life on a bigger scale. At least that's my prayer for any woman reading this book.

It's a practice that I use myself. Every time I work with a woman one-on-one, I ask for her healing to be a universal healing for all women who are going through the same situation. Every time a woman I work with wishes to co-create something important, I open that energy up for all women who desire to co-create the same thing.

Once you experience the meditation exercises, you'll be guided to visualise the entire collective field of all women to receive what you are currently working on.

Download Your Meditations

This book comes with 12 powerful meditations. You can listen to them via the link below:

https://bit.ly/3afPLCM

Let's start then, shall we? Universe, it's your turn!

Hello its Me The Universe

It's ME The Universe

Well, hello there, sparkly, gorgeous soul,

I can't even describe how excited I am to meet you, and even more so, to accompany you throughout this little book and the 11 steps I came up with to help you co-create your desires more powerfully and consistently.

I'll be by your side, every step of the way. (Not in a creepy way, I promise!)

Throughout these steps, you'll learn how to enter into a partnership with me. Don't worry, I won't make you sign a marriage contract and then sue you once I want out. That's not my style. (Also, I don't have patience for writing up contracts.)

We are here to learn how to co-create together, because guess what? You're not meant to do this crazy thing called life alone. You see, not many humans wonder how they can consciously co-create anything with me. I mostly spend my days observing humans praying or wishing for things to happen while not owning up to their part, and then feeling frustrated when I didn't deliver.

But I have a good feeling about you. I really do.

In the next chapters you are going to learn how to own your part in this beautiful dance we shall dance together forever, for the co-creation dance is one that never ends. It's the passionate tango, the patient slow foxtrot, the juicy salsa, the feminine prima ballerina and masculine break-dancer all in one.

Is there anything more marvellous than that? I sure don't think so.

Let's start dancing!

The Universe

#AyeKaramba #Hooray #ChaChaCha

PS: When you humans invented hashtags I went nuts up here. It's my preferred method of communication!

Choose Your Co-Creation Corner

Choose Your Co-Creation Corner

Hello magical pumpkin,

While I'm dictating Lais what to write, I'm observing the autumnal leaves in the parks of Porto and the vineyards in the countryside. Pumpkin season is my favourite human season. I always chuckle when I see how creative humans get once they get hold of a pumpkin. Well, I thought the same about Thanksgiving and the turkey ritual of filling up its derriere with food. What an incredible imagination to have that thought: "Hang on a minute, let's use all this inside space to hide some food in". You humans crack me up, you really do.

Turkeys and pumpkins aside, let's discuss some pre-co-creation business: I want you to dedicate a space at home for our co-creation journey. It can just be a tiny corner somewhere in your home, or if you have enough space and can dedicate a whole room for it, go for it.

Why am I, the Universe, asking you to do this? Because I want you to do the exercises and meditations in this book in that space. Even if it's a temporary space while on holiday, visiting family or friends. Get yourself a dedicated space, and once you have found it, declare in your own mind:

"This is My Co-Creation Corner"

If you have the time (and means) you can make it as cosy and representative as you wish by adding incense, candles, crystals or anything else that brings you into a good mood. But it's not essential.

Go and sit in that corner right now, or, if you are currently not there, visualise sitting in your dedicated space.

I will now, right in this minute, energise that space with a high-level energy field, to which you'll have access during our entire co-creation journey, while reading this book. For some of you it may contain healing. For others, lots of inspiration. For certain individuals it may help with gaining clarity, or it might just feel like a loving energy when you need it the most.

Welcome my energy in. Open yourself up to receive whatever blessing is coming your way—because, trust me—the more you open yourself up during our journey, the more synchronicities, magic and healing will happen along the way.

I also recommend you have a dedicated journal and a pen handy while reading this book. You never know when inspiration will strike, and you might want to write down your feelings and breakthroughs.

Hasta mañana, The Universe **#PumpkinLatteAficionada #CoCreationCornerMagic #AmDieingToHangOut-There**

Pick Your Co-Creation ☆ Goal ☆

✡✩ ♈
Pick Your Co-Creation Goal

Hello, hello, Firecracker,

Let's talk business, you & moi, and let's get down to the nitty gritty of our co-creation journey together. (Please visualise me wearing my best business dress with my Louboutin pumps.)

What, you are shocked? About which part? That I'm wearing female attire or that I love Louboutin? Well, get over it. I am both, female and male, and today I feel more female. And yes, Louboutin was one of the most magical fashion items ever created. (And believe you me, it was I who inspired Monsieur Louboutin with the idea of red soles.)

This book will work best if you only pick one desire to start with. You can always do the 11 steps again with a new goal.

Your desire can be anything from finally convincing your partner to get a puppy, to finding a suitable partner in the first place, or to improve existing relationships in your life— including the most important one: the one you have with yourself. It can be a spiritual wish, in that you wish to improve your communication with the Divine (including me), or something financial in nature, such as a salary increase, or getting that dream job

27

you applied for. Maybe it's health related, and you want to feel more energised again, or to find out the root causes of a chronic illness you have been suffering from and your desire to improve that condition.

Whatever it is, I want you to spend a few moments deciding which co-creation desire you will move forward with during our time together. If you are having a hard time deciding, don't worry. I've got you.

**Download the meditation
"Pick Your Co-Creation Goal."**

You did great! (And so did I!) :D

Love you, Da Universe
**#Louboutinista #GoalsNotDreams
#GoalsSetGoalsMet**

Step 1
Receiving Aligned Inspiration

Step 1: Receiving Aligned Inspiration

Hello darling,

Now we finally get to jam on the really important stuff. I have been waiting for you to read this, for, like, forever (since the Bing Bang to be precise.) Thus, needless to say, this is my favourite step of all!

Step 1 is about opening or strengthening your divine communication channel in order to receive aligned inspiration from me.

You might ask yourself why this is so important in our co-creation process. I would go as far to suggest that if you don't know how to commune with the Divine to receive guidance, signs, or simply just love and healing, then it will be a tough journey for you.

Ignoring my existence, or thinking you can do it alone is like jumping into a truck without knowing how to drive it. You might get it to move eventually, but it will be a hell of a bumpy ride.

Visualising and speaking to me is like a muscle that needs to be built up, just as you tone up your body by regularly investing time in sports. It's the same with your intuition: it needs to be done regularly. In order to deepen the relationship with me, it's just like on Earth with your human friends: the more time you spend with them and build your friendships, the better they become. #AmIRight?

Let me tell you a little secret. No, I'm kidding, I want every single woman on your planet to know this:

When aligned inspiration flows into your awareness, be it in a dream at night, be it an idea downloaded in your meditation, a quick vision you had during your walk in the forest, or a glimpse of a better life while you were crying your eyes out—I want you to know that these ideas are valid. Valid and important. Valid, important and aligned with your soul and higher self. Valid, important, aligned with your soul and higher self and waiting for you to take inspired action on it!

I will work overtime to keep inspiring you, sending you messages, making sure you meet the right people at the right time, and a whole lot of other synchronistic stuff I have up my sleeves.

Your job? To make time to "unbusy" your mind so you can communicate with me and receive guidance all along the way.

Staying in aligned inspiration mode is essential, because your ego, fear-based thoughts and limiting beliefs still have the power to derail you, drain you, make you take U-turns or embrace "wrong" decisions. (Even though there is no such thing as a "wrong" decision in my eyes, of course.) Still, good decisions are made based on aligned inspiration, and some decisions are not. That's what this book is about after all: getting you into co-creation mode, not into "I-can-do-it-alone-mode". But above all, my love bug: As soon as you realise aligned inspiration is flowing into you, your only and most important task is to believe it came through for a reason, and that you must keep working on making your desire a reality.

Let's do a little exercise. Place the palms of your hands on your heart chakra and slowly breathe in and out a few times, relaxing more and more as you do so, and then repeat out loud three times:

"I am ready to open up or strengthen my divine communication channel to its highest potential and for my highest good, so I can communicate with a higher power to receive ongoing inspiration and guidance. I'm ready to start my co-creation journey right here, right now. I believe it's my birthright to making it a physical reality. Dear Universe, I am ready. Let's do this. Thank you, thank you, thank you."

**Do the meditation for Step 1
now and write down your thoughts and feelings
afterwards.**

You did great! (And so did I!) :D

Muchos Love, The Universe
#CoCreationBuddiesForLife #ItsOfficial #Boom!

Step 2
Meet Your Archetype

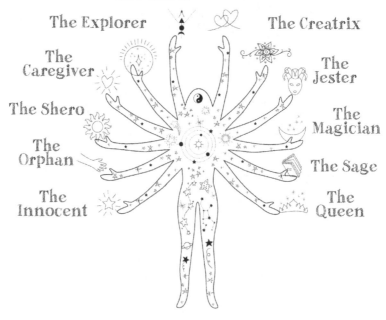

The Rebel

The Lover

The Explorer

The Creatrix

The Caregiver

The Jester

The Shero

The Magician

The Orphan

The Sage

The Innocent

The Queen

Step 2:
Meet Your Archetype

Bonjour ma Queen,

Here we are for step 2: my favourite number and thus my favourite step because it symbolises our special relationship we 2 are building up.

Step 2 is about one of twelve archetypal energies trying to get hold of you to convey important messages and guidance on your co-creation desire. This collective unconscious field of archetypal energies is beaming with inspiration.

Often times you humans think you are alone with your suffering, feeling that no one knows your pain and your struggles; and no one has such a difficult time co-creating something meaningful. Yet, I am here to tell you that your suffering, as well as your specific talents and gifts, are archetypal in nature, felt and lived by millions of others who are working with the same archetypal energy.

Let's do a little exercise. Place the palms of your hands on your heart and slowly breathe in and out a few times, relaxing more and more as you do so, and then repeat out loud three times:

"I am ready to get to know myself on a deeper level, to understand my struggles better, as well as my archetypal gifts and talents, so I can co-create more powerfully. I am ready to meet my archetypal energy. Thank you, thank you, thank you."

I, myself, am nearly dying of anticipation, as believe it or not: I wrote a love note to each and every archetype.

In order to find out which archetype is working through you, close your eyes and ask yourself: "Which archetype has a message for me?"

Ask for a number between 1 and 12 to present itself to you. Maybe you'll see that number visually, maybe you just instinctively know which number it is.

Once you have it, go right to the chapter with that Archetype's number and read your love note.

**Do the meditation for Step 2
now and write down your thoughts and feelings
afterwards.**

See ya in a bit when you find my love note!

The one and only
Universe
**#YouAndMeMakesTwoOfUs #MagicDuo
#TwoPeasInAPod**

1.
The Innocent

Dear Innocent,

You are my favourites, if I may say so. How could you not be, for you brought that innocent energy down from Heaven to Earth with you. You are little angels, are you not? Angels who easily get their wings broken by living through the harsh realities you encounter on Earth.

I want you to repair your wings and fly again. I want your inner magical child to be well and alive, as this is how you access ME and how you get to co-create with me in the best way. Stop adulting for some time. What's up with all that seriousness and anxiousness you are living through? Don't you remember? Don't you remember how you signed up for all of this, but above all, you signed up for it because you wanted to shine an innocent, pure light onto others who might go through dark times?

⚘ ☆ ⚘

When you wish to get into co-creation mode with me, you need to find that innocence and joy again. You need more play and fewer rules, more creativity and imagination versus analysis and facts. And finally, more believing in magic versus rigid and cynical views about people or the world you live in.

Have patience with your co-creation desire: just like handling an infant, the same is true for your project. You need to nurture it, love it, and keep "feeding" it so it can grow into a mature project ready to be birthed.

I am waiting for you and your beautiful energy. Can't wait to meet again and co-create with you, my angel super star!

The Universe

2.
The Orphan

Dear Orphan,

You truly are my favourite archetype because your feelings of abandonment—your core wound so to speak—is not just the abandonment or rejection you experienced early on in your life. It's your original separation from the Divine. You felt abandoned by me, the Universe. And I'm here to tell you that I never abandoned you. You just forgot that you were always part of me and that I dwell deep within your hearts.

In order to co-create with me, I wish for you to see me as your Father/Mother, your true parent who never abandoned you. I ask you to reconnect with your inner divinity and to believe in your own power again, to allow yourself to feel whole. You were never broken to begin with. I needed you to crack open so more of my Light can flood into you.

The day has come: I am here and I love you. And I missed you! So good to have you back! You are a beautiful vessel for the Divine and the more confidence you display in your own power, the stronger this Divine power (Me!) can shine through you.

Let's get to work, shall we?

The Universe

PS I love you, I love you, I love you!

3.
The Shero

Dear Shero,

I know that you know that I told the Innocents and Orphans that they were my favourite ones. If anyone is my favourite for reals, it's YOU! Just look at you. I see all that potential in you and I'm like WOW. And then I'm stupefied each time I see you doubting yourself. #DontDoThat.

   Don't you know the best books and movies are only as good as they are because of the heroes in them? Okay, I must admit I'm a tad bit pissed off that it's mostly men in these roles. Maybe that's why women find it so hard to embark on their own Shero's journey: because of a lack of hero type female leaders.

   Someone great on your planet once said: "Be the change you wish to see in the world."

This world needs more powerful female leaders and we can only have them when the strongest archetype: the Shero, takes her call seriously.

You might not see it yet, but you are a fierce, smart and beautiful warrior with the tools to have a big impact in this world. I promise a massive upleveling in your life once you hear the call and act on it, and keep acting on it without giving up. Do you remember those Duracell bunnies that humans in the advertising industry came up with? That's how I see you. Working endlessly, fearlessly and energetically on your dreams and goals.

In order to co-create with me, you need to find, embrace and embody your inner Shero energy at your greatest capacity. I am here to guide you each step of the way. All you have to do is ask.

Now, let's go and slay some dragons, shall we? I am hungry!

The Universe

PS: Oh, I forgot to mention that some Sheros have to hear several calls, one after the other. If you have been on your journey for a while doing the slaying the dragon thing and are still getting this message, maybe it's time for an even higher calling. You're never truly done.

4.
The Caregiver

Dear Caregiver,

You are by far my most favourite (ever!) I created you because I needed caregivers on Earth who, like me, take care of people, animals or the environment. As I can't do that physically, and because there are many people who don't even believe in my existence, I need YOU to do my work. That's how important you are.

    I cry sometimes, though—I'm not going to lie. That's when we have storms and torrents of rain (so I need to be careful not to weep for too long). But how could I not cry when I see how much energy you put into others and how little time you give yourself to recharge? Sometimes I feel I need to cry on your behalf, because you don't even have time for that: a good cry.

My beautiful soul, in order to co-create with me, I need you to set stricter boundaries and honour your self-care. Literally taking care of yourself is how we both connect best. Because, let me tell you, if your "receiving channel" is switched off, then I can't deliver your co-creations because you are not energetically programmed to receive it.

I will be with you when you take an Epsom salt bath, go for a forest walk, journal or meditate. In those moments you will become your most powerful creator and will have access to all my special powers. (Can't wait to show them to you and to show off a bit, you know?!) You take care of you & I take care of you. Understood?

The Universe

PS: Schedule your "me-times" into your crazy smartphone now, will you?

5.
The Explorer

Dear Explorer,

You are my absolute favourite buddy and co-creator. If I hadn't felt the urge to explore, there wouldn't be the Big Bang, know what I'm saying?

We both see eye to eye. I understand your traveling and exploring urges better than anyone else. Because let's be honest: is there anything more divine than opening ourselves up to new places and energies? Don't we grow incredibly because of this?

I see you struggling, however, in finding your balance and knowing when you need to explore more, or settle and ground for a while, and when it's time to explore your inner world, and when it's time to allow the work you did to integrate.

You are at your most powerful when you feel passionately alive. That's when you find me the easiest. However, I am also with you when you are rooting and grounding somewhere, and I don't think anything less of you when you think you are becoming that "boring old person" who is settling down.

You and I can co-create whenever you feel that passion for internal or external exploration. It's the passion and curiosity that unites us. Get passionate, get curious and I'll be there.

The Universe

PS: I love nothing more than accompanying you through your explorations as I explore myself through your adventures as well...

6.
The Rebel

Dear Rebel,

I know you are in rebelling mode and probably rebelling right now to be put into a label such as an archetype. Ha! #AmIRight? But this is precisely what makes you my most favourite archetype since the invention of archetypes.

I created you so you would incarnate on Earth and talk some sense into some of your fellow human beings. Because—really? Nobody listens to me. You are my speakers, sharing a fierce divine truth with others. You are showing what's not working. I love you for your no-bullshit energy. You are my Universal paratroopers, being sent to wake people the eff up. Yes, that's me cursing and rebelling. (I'm quite good at that too, you know?!) I love how I can just be myself around you. Everyone else seems to think I am all-loving, patient and vanilla, when I'm not!

However, I see many of you rebels overdoing this. I see so much anger, even hatred when it gets taken too far. I see you not being able to focus on anything else anymore and forget about all the beautiful things your planet has to offer too.

You and I can co-create together very powerfully when you focus just as much on what's going well in your life—and on your planet in general—and when you rebel through the lens of love and non-violence. That passion you have to make this planet a better place is what I LOVE. It's that energy you need to be in so I can come and find you and meet you at that level, as that's the level I play at.

The Universe

PS: I also love you when you realise you are just a human being and can't save the world all the time and spend time on less mundane things, such as passionately washing the dishes (without breaking them!)

7.
The Lover

Dear Lover,

Probably you are thinking I love all the other archetypes more than you, but far from it. You are Divine Love manifested into a human body. From all the archetypes, you are the one who has the capacity to love the most and to learn about all the different kinds of love: the messy ones, the unrequited ones, the overbearing or controlling ones, the ones where you accidentally dated a narcissist.

All of this just happened for you so you could embark on a much-needed self-love journey. Have you already been on it? Then the message is that you are ready to go even deeper, lovebug!

You are at your most powerful to co-create with me when you radiate self-love out of every one of your pores (and hey—your pores look beautiful, no need to use heavy makeup to make them disappear!) When you vibrate at a high level of love, you and I become one and I will be your faithful servant, making your wishes come true.

The Universe

PS: Show me that beautiful smile of yours right now. I'm sooo addicted to it. Yes, that's the one right there. Keep going. :D

8.
The Creatrix

Dear Creatrix,

Who is the original creatrix? Yep, that's right: Me, the Universe. I wish I had the time and space to write about with how much love I created your galaxy, your world, and every human being currently living on Earth. But what I really, really want you to know is that the number one archetype I needed to be present, was the Creatrix. (I'm tearing up as I write this.)

What would this world be without your creations, your originality and your creativity? Thank you for everything you have created thus far. Thank you for pouring your soul into your creations—whether you deem yourself successful or not. Whether that creation has been seen by anyone else other than you or not. I see you. I love you and all of your creations so very much.

I also see you suffering a great deal because of your perfectionism, always trying to produce a perfect piece of art. Dare to fail, not that there is any failure in my eyes. Daring to enjoy every failure equally as every success is the only thing I care about—that you are working with creation energy, the most important energy there is. Don't you agree?

You can most powerfully co-create with me when you enjoy the Divine communion between You and Me while creating. I am right there with you with every word you write, and every stroke you use with your paint brush. I am there with every creative thought you ever think, for I AM that creative thought. Also don't forget that sometimes, in order to materialise your desires, you first need to allow destruction and chaos to occur in your life to make room for new opportunities and creations. I am right there with you then as well, as destruction and creation is all the same energy and all Divine in my eyes.

PS: Let's go and finish that beautiful piece of art we started together...

9.
The Jester

Dear Jester,

Oh, how many times did I catch myself laughing and tearing up because of your silliness, which accidentally caused some drizzling downpour. I wouldn't be the powerful Creatrix I am without YOU in my life.

You always crack me up the mostest, which is why you are my favourite archetype by far. Also, there is no other archetype who lives so much in the present moment as you do. And living in the present moment is the one important thing I am trying to teach all these human beings. And you are the one teaching it. Thank you.

You are a healer, whether you are aware of it or not. You bring light-hearted healing energy to anyone going through a rough time. And how Divine is that?

Some people might think you are superficial for never showing your true colours. But I know that's far from the truth. I know all about your difficult upbringing and the many times you suffered in silence. Usually, those who laugh the loudest are the ones who experienced the most pain in their lives, too. Isn't it so?

However, I see you struggling sometimes, all alone, not allowing anyone to hold space for you. I wish I could, but I feel you block me out too, in your moments of deep despair. My wish for you is that you keep your light-hearted outlook on life, but also learn how to speak about your problems and find the humans who can hold that space for you. I am right there, too, when you need someone to listen to you. I recently won the "Best listener award in the entire Universe".

You and I co-create together through your light-heartedness, your inner child energy and your playfulness. Crack up a joke, smile or laugh, I am right there with you. But as I said before, you are just as Divine when you struggle and have pain. Just don't hide it from yourself and others, as that energy sort of blocks our co-cre-ation process, and I most definitely don't want that.

HA-HA-HA & warm regards and all that,

The Universe

PS: Two elephants meet a totally naked guy. After a while one elephant says to the other: "I really don't get how he can feed himself with that thing!"

10.
The Magician

Dear Magician,

I won't tell you how you are my favourite Archetype because you can see through my bullshit and any other illusions. Being spiritually aware, you of course know that I love everyone the same, with Oneness being such an important lesson and all.

However, more than any other Archetype, you manage to build that bridge between the Divine (Me) and humankind. You literally bring my Divinity to Earth by being who you are. So how could you not be THE MOST important archetype in the history of all archetypes?

What fascinates me the most is how you transcended your pain and your shadow into being an important carrier of light: lighting up other people's path who can't yet see the light at the end of their tunnel.

Every time you felt pain and struggled, I was right there with you, holding you.

Every time you shine your light, I am with you.

I am always with you, even in the times you think I am not.

If you are reading this while being in a dark tunnel, let me shine the brightest light for you right now and watch out for my gorgeous face at the end of the tunnel. Can you spot me with my big grin?

You can most powerfully co-create with me when you shine like the biggest lighthouse in the world: the one in Jeddah at 436 feet. When you are at your most powerful self and believe you are beautiful and worthy of love, I am right there with you.

Simsalabim, it's Abracadabra time, me thinks...

The Universe

PS: Go and listen to the song "I am Light" by India Arie.

11.
The Sage

Dear Sage,

You probably want some facts and extensive research into why you are my most favourite archetype. (Including facts proving my existence). You are my favourite archetype because you are the least one to need me. The least one to seek my attention, like some of the other archetypes. You are content on your own, aren't you? So much so that you might take it too far sometimes.

I see you isolating yourself a lot, staying away from social crowds and doing your own thing. I see how you easily lose yourself when surrounded by noise and other people, and how you prefer your own company with books to study, research to be done, and facts to be analysed.

You are so busy in your mind that you don't even feel lonely, or when you do, you concentrate on your studying. But eventually loneliness pours out of every one of your cells so strongly, that it nearly overwhelms me witnessing this.

I want you to share your wisdom and knowledge on an even bigger scale, making sure you grow and allow yourself to become the expert in a field you know you can be, or already are. My vision for you includes opening up your heart more to balance out the mind activity.

And there, in that heart-space, in-between all your thoughts, you will find me. WOW! We just connected. I felt it. You felt it. What a wonderful connection. Let's keep it, for that's how we most powerfully co-create together. In that space between thoughts, when all you feel is passion and an insatiable thirst for learning (and now also that curious moment when you wonder who I really am and what I can bring to the table.)

I'll always be there waiting for you.

The Universe

PS: Wow, just wow! I'm still feeling dizzy from that connection we made. What an honour to connect with an old soul such as yourself! Truly Wowzers!

12.
The Queen

Dear Queen,

Once you fully embody the energy of a Queen, I love you the most from all archetypes. How couldn't I? You are sort of in my face then. Shimmering with delicious confidence and funky leadership energy, which is the yummiest of all energies, really!

Not only do you have what it takes to transcend your own limitations, but you will outgrow yourself by helping other human beings transcend their limitations. WOW! Isn't that precisely what this world needs right now? Strong female leaders leading from their hearts?

(Give me a second here as I am weeping... it's just too beautiful. I have been waiting for this moment, for, like, forever. Okay, time is different up here, but you get my point.)

When you rise, all other women rise too. I can't even put into words how much I love you and how important you are. I do see all your struggles too, of course. Rising as a strong female leader isn't for the faint hearted. There are so many obstacles to overcome, and so many hurdles on the way, aren't there?

I want you to know it's important you keep going, even when you fail once. Even when you fail twice. Stand up again, straighten your crown and keep going. Do not mistake the heaviness of your path with the Universe (Me) putting obstacles into your way. It's not me. It's the unjust systems that are currently still a reality on your planet.

I want to co-create with you so badly. And we do so when you stand straight, crown on your head, smile on your face, and when determination energy radiates all around you. I am right next to you, then, reading your every wish like a lovesick Genie.

I Heart You,

The Universe

PS: You are my Queen of Hearts!

Step 3
Release Blockages
From Your Past

past lives & karma

negative womb memories

ancestral baggage

limiting beliefs & fears

repressed emotions

Step 3:
Release Blockages From Your Past

Dear funky Time-Traveler,

Here we are with Step 3: my favourite and most intensive one, as there is a ton of baggage from your past that might be blocking your current co-creation efforts.

You see, as long as you haven't cleared the energetic junk, accumulated because of past traumas, your co-creation energy consists of low, stuck, maybe even blocked energy. This will prevent you from co-creating powerfully and consistently. And what's worse: you might be sabotaging yourself. There is nada I can do from up here when I see that happening. All I pray for is for you to find a way to release all that baggage once and for all.

You might be wondering what I am talking about, specifically. I know you humans always need to understand everything in detail. #LemmeTryMyBest

The baggage you might be carrying from the past may contain the energy of repressed or suppressed emotions you never allowed yourself to feel, let alone clear away. In case you are an empath, you also might be carrying other people's unresolved emotional baggage, including that of your parents and ancestors. You might be holding on to negative womb memories and even past life traumas from previous incarnations.

You might be holding on to limiting beliefs and fears or might have taken on your parent's and ancestor's limiting beliefs around love, career, health or abundance in general, and then continued to build on top of that limiting worldview. All of this may become a self-fulfilling prophecy if you don't release it.

I am quite aware of your past traumas and what you need to release before you get into powerful co-creation mode. If you allow yourself to surrender, I promise I'll help you remove that heavy energetic junk you no longer need to carry around.

I am quite aware of your past traumas and what you need to release before you get into powerful co-creation mode. If you allow yourself to surrender, I promise I'll help you remove that heavy energetic junk you no longer need to carry around.

Let's do a little exercise. Place the palms of your hands on your heart and slowly breathe in and out a few times, relaxing more and more as you do so, and then repeat the below out loud three times: come in.

"I am ready to clear my old energetic baggage and let go of stuck energy, whether my own or that of other people. I am ready to co-create more powerfully and consistently by increasing my energy levels. I deserve to heal. I deserve to release what's not mine to carry. I deserve to release the old to make space for more love, health and abundance to come and find me. I am ready, Universe, let's do this. Thank you, thank you, thank you."

You are ready for meditation for Step 3.
Write down your thoughts and feelings
afterwards.

Love, love, love you brave time-traveler!

#BuckleUpButtercup, #WeAreGoingOnARide
#DivineBaggageRemover

Step 4
Master Your
Now-Moments

⇠Blessed→

⇠Thankful→

⇠Self Love→

Step 4: Master Your Now-Moments

Hello aspiring Buddhalicious soul,

Uh, have we reached Step 4 yet? It's my favourite one! Is there anything more magical than the present moment?

The only time that truly matters in terms of your co-creation power is your Now-Moment. Being present in the Now, paying attention to your breath, practicing gratitude for what is, acceptance for the things that didn't go according to plan, compassion of self and others, and taking responsibility for your thoughts and actions: This all only takes place in your Now-Moments.

If you learned one thing out of this book, and one thing only, I really wish it were this one:

You are a powerful creatrix. You are only a powerful creatrix, however, in your Now-Moments, not in the past, nor in the future, but right here, right now.

Let's talk about gratitude for a hot minute. Gratitude is my soul-food, like chocolate or that delicious smelling French baguette of yours. I get high on gratitude: it's my favourite drug of all (not that I tried any—ahem!) But more precisely, I get high on the frequency of gratitude. This emotion, together with very few others, is one of the highest vibrations there is. And what's more: you can only feel grateful in the present. Gratitude catapults you into your Now-Moment at lightning speed.

If I had the chance to co-create with a woman who doesn't appreciate the gift of life and what life has to offer—and that includes the good, the bad and the ugly—or with a woman who helps me get high, you know who I will pick, right?

Gratitude is my favourite hors d'oeuvres, followed by self-compassion as a main dish. I often see you putting yourself down and being so incredibly hard on yourself. Ugh, let's not go there, as this gives me the heebie-jeebies. You know what you are? You are a beautiful canvass of art in progress, that's who you are.

Me, the Universe, never judges you. You can do no wrong in my book. So many of your religions focus heavily on what happens when human beings "sin" and create fear-based concepts, such as hell, where you will be forever tortured. Clearly these religions haven't really met me, have they? I could never judge you, nor condemn you. How could I? You are part of me, and I am part of you, and there are no mistakes in my eyes. You are an absolutely divine and beautiful soul. Always have been, always will be. Have I already told you how much I love you? Well, I do! Now more than ever.

Self-compassion, just like gratitude, is only possible in your Now-Moments. It includes learning how to become more mindful of the negative self-talk, and becoming more aware of the consequences of your internalised judgement energy. The more you judge yourself, the more judgement energy you build up and project onto others too. You will easily feel triggered by other people who have the traits you deeply judge within yourself, while not always noticing that these people are merely acting as a mirror to the unhealed parts within yourself.

Let's do a little exercise. Place the palms of your hands on your heart and slowly breathe in and out a few times, relaxing more and more as you do so. Repeat the sentences below out loud three times.

"I am ready to embrace my Now-Moments on a deeper level and to allow myself to become the creatrix I know I can be. I am ready to invite in more gratitude, self-compassion, and take responsibility for my thoughts and actions. I am Divine Love incarnated on Earth. I am always loved. I am a beautiful child of the Universe. I come from Love and I return to Love. Dear Universe, please guide me along the way and show me when I deviate from this path. Help me find my way back to my present moment, the most precious moment there is. Thank you, thank you, thank you."

Wow, just wow. See what we did here? You have been in the present moment, deeply mindful, for at least a few minutes while reading this. Feel free to repeat this affirmation with me daily, if you'd like.

You are now ready for meditation for Step 4. Write down your thoughts and feelings afterwards.

Sending you the love of the entire Universe, the stars and the moons.

Your Universe

PS: Instead of bingeing on Netflix, let's binge-sing together to Alanis Morisette "Thank U", for she is one of my many missionaries sent down to Earth to spread the message of gratitude.

#GratitudeIsAnAttitude #GettingIntoRhyming-Here #CompassionIsMyFashion

Step 5
Make Your
Cosmic Order

Step 5: Make Your Cosmic Order

Hello super star, I missed you!

Here we are for Step 5. It's the most beautiful chapter I have lined up for you in this book: our little cosmic party. It's about engaging me in your plans. Let me explain via an easy example. Let's pretend your co-creation desire is to find the perfect home for you.

During Step 1 you and I connected, and you told me about your desire of finding the perfect home. Let's call it a "blueprint" of an idea.

Step 2, then, was about finding which archetypal energy you are working with, and making sure you use the strengths of that archetype to increase your co-creation power. Let's pretend it was the Explorer Archetype. If that's your archetype, it might mean you have some limiting beliefs or fears around settling somewhere long-term, or signing binding contracts. Just because everyone dreams of having their own house with a garden and a picket fence doesn't mean that this is your thing. But once you've released any of that and embraced the Explorer's strengths, such as being great at exploring new neighbourhoods, and being open for new areas to live, you gave me the chance to look for something outside of the box for you.

Step 3 was about making sure you heal the blockages from the past that could prevent you from finding and receiving this amazing house. Maybe you had some traumas in your past in the home where you grew up. Perhaps your fears of commitment are showing up due to old wounds from abandonment. Or it may be that one or more of your ancestors lost their homes during wartime or the aftermath of economic recessions, and you are still carrying that burden and that fear for them.

Step 4 was about making sure you spend more time in the present moment to keep that co-creation energy flowing between the two of us, and making sure you practice more self-compassion and gratitude.

Step 5 now is about giving to that house. You can tell me about the wall colours and decoration, furniture and appliances, wallpaper and a walk-in wardrobe (yes, I know you love these things). See what I mean? It's about you telling me how you wish to fill that blueprint with your own ideas, visions and feelings.

I want you to take your co-creation idea and dream up the rest that you desire by using all your sensorial means: visions, feelings, hearing, taste and touch.

In this case it involves visualising what the perfect home could look like, how many rooms it would have, what kind of kitchen, and whether it has a garden. You would focus on the emotion of what it feels like to have a perfect home to come back to every day after work, and what it feels like to wake up in your new bedroom. You would concentrate on the sounds within the house, such as the sound of the hoover when you are cleaning, or the noise your partner is making while cooking up something delicious in the kitchen. In fact, you could even focus on the taste of that meal, the sparkly wine you drink with it, the incense you burn. And last but not least, you focus on touch. Imagine what the walls feel like, or the carpets on the floor, what your blanket feels like, or the hot shower on your skin.

Let's do a little exercise. Place the palms of your hands on your heart chakra and slowly breathe in and out a few times, relaxing more and more as you do so. Repeat the sentences below out loud three times.

"I am a powerful co-creator, and I rejoice in using my sensorial skills to engage the Universe in my dreams and desires. I love feeding the Universe with the details of what it is I desire. I love getting into the feeling of already having received what it is I desire."

Easy peasy? You are ready for meditation for Step 5. Write down your thoughts and feelings afterwards.

You're a star!

Rock on,

Your Universe

#LetsStartTheSensorialParty #DjUniverseInDaHouse #WoopWoop

Step 6
Abracadabra-ing
It Up

I am worthy of love

My voice & my message matters

I am Divinity in a physical body

Step 6:
Abracadabraing it up

Hello fellow magicians,

Is there anything more marvellous than a step that works with the magic of ABRACABRA? I saw how your jaw just dropped, wondering whether I'm on hallucinogens. Lemme explain this better.

Let's talk about the power of words. At the beginning, there was an inspiration, a thought. The next most powerful action is to voice that thought, because words are creative, even more creative and powerful than thoughts.

Inspired thoughts, visualisations and the resulting emotions are only the first basic steps in our co-creation process. Using the power of words will help you co-create more powerfully. And this is what ABRACADABRA is all about. It's not just something magicians say to pull a rabbit out of their hat. The word comes from the very first language you humans spoke: Aramaic.

"Avra kadavra" in Aramaic means "it will be created in my words." Let's repeat this for more impact: **It will be created in my words.**

My magic lovebird, pay attention to every word you use when co-creating. Words have immense power and they can be the reason you fail our co-creation project, or be the enabling force to co-create with record speed.

Putting your inspired ideas and emotions into words, be it written or spoken out loud, (or sung or chanted for that matter) have a profound way of accelerating the physical manifestations of your desires.

Let's do a little exercise. Place the palms of your hands on your throat chakra and slowly breathe in and out a few times, relaxing more and more as you do so. Repeat the sentences below out loud three times.

"I am a powerful co-creator and I use my words carefully. I choose to use kind words when speaking about myself and others. My words, both spoken and written, are as powerful as they ever will be. Every affirmation or mantra I create and speak out loud has the capacity to energise my co-creation desire a hundredfold."

You are ready for meditation for Step 6. Write down your thoughts and feelings afterwards.

I Heart You!

The Universe

#MagiciansLife #Wordsmith #Wordsmatter

Step 7

Switch On
Your Receiving Channel

Step 7: Switch On Your Receiving Channel

Hello magical stardust,

Are you ready for Step 7? This one for sure is my favourite one because without this step you would block yourself from receiving the wonderful gifts I simply CANNOT wait to send you. **#ImpatienceOverload**

I'm talking about your feelings of self-worth. I see so many of you feeling you are not good enough, not smart enough, not knowledgeable enough, or, in a nutshell, not worthy of receiving what it is you truly want.

Each time a thought of "not enough" pops into your head, you are telling me that you are not worthy of receiving something better, and I can't, therefore, send it to you. I can only send you what you are energetically ready to receive.

Let me tell you something, my magic owl. You are worthy in my eyes, always, and it's about time you believe this to be true. You are worthy to receive your wildest dreams.

#AndSomeMore

Repeat my favourite mantra I came up with just for you. Place the palms of your hands on your heart chakra and slowly breathe in and out a few times, relaxing more and more as you do so. Repeat the sentences below out loud three times.

"I am worthy of divine love and infinite abundance. I am worthy of being loved with all my flaws and imperfections because I am a Divine child of the Universe, and nothing I do or don't do can change the unconditional love flowing towards me. I open myself up towards infinite love and acceptance. I joyfully receive love and abundance each day, every hour and every second. I am a magnet for Divine love. I am worthy of healing my heart from any pain I held on to for far too long. Please send me some healing to open my heart further. Thank you, Universe, for sending me a sign as soon as I forget about my worthiness so I can realign myself again. Thank you, thank you, thank you."

Hey, I was tearing up while you were doing this exercise. I feel that your worthiness and capacity to receive my gifts just increased. Can you feel it too?

Last but not least, please listen to "Worthy" by India Arie now.

You are ready for meditation for Step 7. Write down your thoughts and feelings afterwards.

I Heart You Mucho!

The Universe

#YouMatter #IHeartYouSomeMore #SwitchOnYourReceivingChannel

Step 8
Give what you wish to Receive

Step 8:
Give What You Wish To Receive

Hey there. my favourite human,

Step 8 is my favourite step because I'm in love with the number 8. Doesn't it look so pretty? I love how it symbolises infinity, which you all are: infinite, limitless beings.

If Step 7 was all about receiving, Step 8 is all about giving, giving, giving. If it were up to me, this would be the only spiritual law that mattered. Oh wait, it is up to me. Lemme see if I can change things around up here.

Is there anything more beautiful than a human being emitting the energy of giving? It's no secret by now, I hope, that in order to receive that which you desire, you need to be an energetic match to receive it. And what better way to be an energetic match than to give to others the very thing you wish to receive yourself?

In a nutshell, the spiritual "give to receive law" is the opposite of the law of cause and effect, or karma. The saying "what you reap is what you sow," works both ways.

If you enable others to grow, to become a better version of themselves, make them feel loved and cared for, you will be taken care of by the same energy in return.

Thus, if you are looking for love, be love and be happy for those who have found it.

If you're looking for an upleveling in your career, help others succeed too and celebrate with anyone who upleveled their career in any way.

If you desire to attract helpful people into your life, be helpful and appreciate this trait in others.

I don't want you to over-give to others, though, I want you to give to yourself just as much, if not more. I cannot co-create with you if you are exhausted, depleted and burned out, as we won't be equal partners then. You wouldn't want me to show up cranky, tired and in a foul mood, would you? And believe me, when my mood gets foul, you don't want to be anywhere near me!

Anyhoo, enough about foul moods, they stink! It's time for a little affirmation. Sit down comfortably and place your hands on your heart chakra. Take a few deep breaths in and set the intention to work on your "giving energy".

Repeat the mantra below three times.

"I love to give and open myself up to receive it back one hundredfold. I enjoy the process of giving. I open myself up to give that which I desire to receive and ask the Universe to guide me and show me how. I ask for the Universe to show me how I can improve my giving, so I am an energetic match to that which I desire to receive. Thank you, thank you, thank you."

Well done! You are ready for meditation for Step 8. Write down your thoughts and feelings afterwards.

Your Giving Universe

#GiveMoreJudgeLess #ButFillYourOwnCupFirst #Givernatrix

Step 9
Taking Inspired
Action

Step 9 : Taking Inspired Action

Hola inspired little witches,

Finally! Step 9, here we come! Up until now we discussed all the fluffy stuff. It's time to get to the nitty gritty. Thus, needless to say, it's my favourite step of all times, because imagine if I hadn't taken inspired action—the Big Bang would never have happened, would it? Just my thoughts and visualisations alone wouldn't have created the world you live in. See where I am going with this?

I get ecstatic when I see you creating vision boards or spending time on writing things down you wish to create into existence. But when I see you going back to normal life and not taking any "real" action towards your goal, I get a soury taste in my mouth. I see so many of you earthlings receiving the inspiration I carefully send you. I wish you could see yourselves when that happens: the most beautiful light builds up around you, your heart chakra expands, and your soul comes alive. It's so beautiful to watch from up here.

Sadly, shortly after, that sparkle in your eye vanishes. You decided it's not the right time to pursue this dream or that many other things need to fall into place first: that it's just a chimaera, a silly construct of your

You see, when I make sure my divine nuggets flow into your awareness, I want you to act on them. Even if it's just a tiny step in that direction, followed by yet another tiny step. And another one after that. Oooh, how I love your tiny step moments. That's when I will step in and support you fully by inspiring you with all the next steps to take.

Let's do a little exercise: Place the palms of your hands on your solar plexus chakra and repeat the below affirmation aloud three times:

"I am ready to take inspired action. I allow the right ideas to flow into my awareness and trust that the inspiration I receive is divine, knowing that taking inspired action will propel me forward. I am ready to step out of my comfort zone and work with high-level co-creation energy by doing my part in the co-creation process. I trust that once I take a step into the right direction, the Universe will show me each step at a time. I am opening myself up for timely guidance and inspirational ideas, and I am ready to work on my willpower to make my desires a reality."

**And now, go, go, go: Jot down some inspired
actions you could take. I'm cheering you on!
You are ready for meditation for Step 9.
Write down your thoughts and feelings
afterwards.**

Truly yours forever,

The Universe

**#InspirationNuggetsAlert #WhenInspirationHits
#TakingActionRightNow
#WhatAreYouWaitingFor #TickTock**

Step 10
The Magic Of
Synergies

Step 10 : The Magic Of Synergies

Bonjour les Co-creatrices,

Finally we get to Step 10 and talking about what really matters! Synergies. My favourite word of all.

Synergies are of utmost importance because if you wish to co-create something magnificent, most likely you won't manage it by yourself. Isn't the co-creation process the most beautiful synergy there is? You and me, creating something together. If you asked me to explain in simple terms what synergy is from my point of view, I would say:

Synergy is the result of an energy that expands through cooperation, thus elevating the potential of an outcome for everyone involved. As you know, I am all about expansion and I love nothing more than to expand through our co-operation.

I operate entirely through synergy. So does nature.

In order to co-create with me, I ask you to reflect on your energy. Are you someone who values teamwork and includes others? Are you someone who believes in the power of achieving something greater together? Or do you go through life as a "lonely wolf",
wanting to achieve everything by yourself without any help or cooperation?

Because let me tell you: The relationships you foster on Earth correspond to the relationship the two of us will be able to have. Not because I resent or judge you. I operate in vibration and frequency, remember? When I feel "lonely wolf" energy, the only thing I can send you is more of the same: situations where you get to act out the lonely wolf scenario you created for yourself. If I feel competition energy, I will send you more competitive people who are not interested in teamwork or collaboration.

If you are ready to take your co-creation goal to the next level and uplevel our relationship, here is a little affirmation for you to repeat three times. Place the palms of your hands on your naval chakra and repeat:

"I am the Universe's right hand on Earth. Without my help the Universe could never create a big impact. The Universe needs me to do my part, just as much as I need the Universe to help me create what I deem important in my life. We are equal co-creators and equally important in our co-creation project. I am ready to open myself up towards an even more powerful synergistic co-operation between me and the Universe, and between me and other human beings. I am ready to let go of synergies which are no longer in my highest good and which lower my energy versus uplevels me."

I had shivers running down my spine when you cited these sentences. I felt your request for deep co-operation. Needless to say, I love you more today than I ever have— what an expansion of love I get to experience because of you. Thank you!

You are ready for meditation for Step 10. Write down your thoughts and feelings afterwards.

Yours truly, Universe

#SynergyBombAhead #Boom #UplevelingOurSynery #ImOnIt #LetsDoThis

Step 11
The Art Of
Letting Go

Step 11 : The Art Of Letting Go

Hello my Love Unicorn,

Oh no, is this step 11 already? No way! I am not prepared to say goodbye yet. I'm aware this is somewhat ironic, given that Step 11 is all about the art of letting go. This, for once, is NOT my favourite step! **#Boo!**

My love, what a journey we have been on. I loved every single minute we spent together. I felt every single time you opened up your heart towards me and built up your faith in me. And even when you doubted yourself (or me), I was there right by your side, loving you.

Because ultimately, this was my main goal with this book: connecting with you on a much deeper level.

I am also going to reveal an important secret:

The having of something is not as important as the journey it took you to get into this "having it" state. Everything can be taken away from you again in one brief blink. So enjoy the co-creation process, the present moment, the journey of getting there just as if you already had it, as that is all you have control over: the mindset with which you create, the feelings of gratitude while creating it and your presence in each Now- Moment of creation.

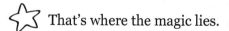 That's where the magic lies.

 That's where transformation happens.

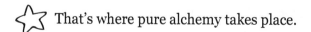 That's where pure alchemy takes place.

That's where your potential for growth lies.

That's where you can challenge yourself.

Co-create because you LOVE co-creating. Let go of the expectations and the attachment to your desired outcome. Achieving your desired goal is only the beginning of yet another co-creation journey.

Well, now it's time to say good-bye to your co-creation project. You did your part, and now it's my time to shine...*cough cough.* No pressure, right?

You fed me intensively with your vision, desires and inspired actions. Now it's my time to bring your creations to life by helping you make it a physical reality. I am not going to share all my secrets on how I do this, but know one thing for sure:

#ImOnIt

All you have to do is to keep the belief that your co-creation desire is being worked on. In order to increase the energy of faith, please place your hands on your heart chakra and repeat the affirmation below three times:

"Dear Universe, I love you and the relationship we have been building. I open myself up to receiving even more of your love and allow myself to tap into your infinite abundance. I have complete faith in your abilities and allow you to work your magic in divine timing for my and everyone else's highest good. My desires, dreams and goals are now in your hands. Thank you, thank you, thank you."

Wow, wow, wowie, I loved it. With these words I'll go get working in my cosmic kitchen. I have all the ingredients I need to start working on our delicious cosmic soup.

You are ready for your final meditation for Step 11. Write down your thoughts and feelings afterwards.

Love you forever and ever,

Your bff,

The Universe

#BFFForever #NoPressureNoDiamonds #DetachedElegantly

11 Step Overview Recap

Receiving Aligned Inspiration

Step 1 helped you hone your intuitive powers to commune with the Universe. This step was about receiving absolute clarity, tips and guidance around your co-creation desire, You increased your co-creation energy by building up more faith and trust in a higher, divine power.

Step 2

Meet Your Archetype

Step 2 helped you connect to your Archetypal energy. You gained a deeper understanding about your potential "shadows" and how these might be working against you when co-creating your desire. You also gained better awareness about your potential "light attributes," a/k/a the strengths you have to co-create faster and more powerfully.

Release Blockages From Your Past

In step 3 you learned how to release energetic blockages from your past that were keeping you stuck in negative patterns and preventing you from co-creating your desires. This enabled you to work with a higher-level energy to pursue your dreams.

Master Your Now-Moments

Step 4 enabled you to master and elevate your present life. Now that you have cleared away old and stuck energy you no longer need, you have more energy to focus on the daily important rituals, behaviours and mindset shifts. You will practice gratitude and develop more compassion towards self and others.

Make Your Cosmic Order

Step 5 was about telling the Universe in detail what exactly it is you desire with the use of all of your senses. Now that you have increased your co-creation energy by removing old stuck energy and are able to master your Now-Moments better, you are in great energetic shape to make your "cosmic orders".

Step 6

Abracadabra-ing It Up: The Power Of Words

Step 6 was about learning about the power of the word via affirmations and how you can use them to infuse your co-creation desire with even more high-level energy.

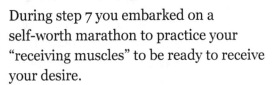 **Step 7**

Switch On Your Receiving Channel

During step 7 you embarked on a self-worth marathon to practice your "receiving muscles" to be ready to receive your desire.

 Step 8

Give What You Wish To Receive

In step 8 you learned about how you can practice giving in a way that's relevant to your co-creation desire in order to further increase your co-creation energy.

Step 9

Taking Inspired Action

Step 9 was about taking inspired action consistently towards your co-creation desire. Now that you have built up an incredible amount of co-creation energy, the inspired actions you will take, will be fuelled by that high-level energy.

Step 10

The Magic of Synergies

In step 10 you learned about the importance of synergies, the most important being the one you have been building up with the Universe in order to co-create your desire more quickly and powerfully. You learned how to connect to the Higher Selves of inspiring figures (dead or alive) who already achieved what it is you desire in your co-creation.

Step 11

The Art Of Letting Go

In step 11 you learned about the art of letting go of your co-creation desire, as well as allowing the Universe to take over while having faith that your desire is being co-created.

FAQ

 I finished reading the book and did all the meditations. Now what do I do?

Even though Step 11 is all about the art of letting go and asks you to step aside to let the Universe take charge, it doesn't mean that your involvement should come to a complete halt. I recommend that you check in with yourself at least once a week to ask: "Which of the 11 steps should I focus on this coming week?"

A number between 1 and 11 will come to you intuitively. That's the step you should focus on. Let's say you got number 2. Step 2 is about meeting your archetype to receive messages during the meditation and reading your love note from the Universe. Make time during the coming week to re-read your love note and to listen to the meditation to re-connect with your archetypal energy. Most likely you will receive further guidance, healing or tips.

If you are going through tumultuous times, I recommend checking in daily or every few days.

Tip: If you don't trust that the number you receive is the right one, you can also cut out 11 pieces of paper and number them from 1–11, shuffle them and pick one at random to get your number.

What happens with my relationship with the Universe once I finish the book?

While reading the book and doing the meditations, you will have massively opened your channelling and intuitive channels so that the Universe will have easier access to you. Pay attention to inspiring thoughts and ideas coming into your awareness. Make it a habit to immediately jot down your dreams upon awakening as the Universe likes to send messages through our dreamscape. Be open for synchronicities and signs along the way.

I recommend keeping the communication between you two going. Meditate regularly to connect to the Universe even for topics outside your co-creation goal: you can share your burdens and worries with the Universe, or just share how your day was or tell the Universe how grateful you feel and what for.

 I am having a hard time visualising and communicating with the Universe. Can you help?

The trick is to have fun and to imagine what the Universe could look like. Some people see an energy, others a colour, and some people see an actual figure, while others prefer to visualise their Higher Self, i.e. an older and wiser version of yourself. There is no right or wrong as to how the Universe presents itself to you. Maybe you don't see anything but just feel its presence. Everything goes.

In terms of communication: be patient. If you are an absolute beginner and are just developing your intuition, you might only receive a few words, an image or very limited information during your conversation. The communication drastically improves the more you practice. Don't give up, keep trying!

 How do I know that I am communicating with the Universe versus just with myself?

Having a conversation is the easy part. The difficult part is to trust and have faith that what is coming through is indeed from the Universe and not just you making it up. The important guideline here is that the Universe or any higher evolved force will never talk negatively, or seem angry or disappointed. These are sure signs that your ego-mind took over and you are having nothing but a negative self-talk. The Universe is always loving, patient, wise and humorous.

Should you have allowed negative self-talk to happen, don't worry. Take a few moments to breathe and re-start the meditation again.

 A lot came up for me during Step 3: Release Blockages From Your Past. I feel I need more help. What do I do?

It sounds like you have been carrying a lot of baggage, just like I did when I started on my self-healing journey. The realisation that there is a lot you need to release is a great first step on your healing journey. Of course, no book will be able to help someone release lifetimes of baggage: healing takes time and effort. I recommend you find a professional to help you, be it a coach, a healer, a counsellor or a therapist. I work with a lot of women one-on-one who require more help. You can find more information on working with me on my website: http://abundantchicks.com

 I have released so much negative energy during this journey. However, now I feel it's lingering around my house and is bringing down the energy. What do you recommend?

It's an absolute certainty that the energy you release during self-development work will remain in your home, and the more you have released, the more that energy might bring the energy of your home down. As a professional Space Clearing Expert, I recommend a few different things:

 Burn white sage in all your rooms. That should help with most of the negative energy.

 Meditate and visualise a swirl of white light passing through each room. Set the intention that this white light will take away all stuck and negative energy.

 Invite in positive energy through an intention like, "I am ready to receive high-level energy into my home."

 Have a bath and add sea salt to it. This will clear your own energy.

If none of these seem to help, you can always ask a professional space clearing expert to assist. I do these via distance and you can find out more about my service with the link below:
http://abundantchicks.com/spaceclearing

How do I know I made progress once I finish Step 11?

Different people will get different results out of this book. If one or more of the following points happened, you made progress:

 You received at least one "wisdom nugget" – inspiration or guidance. during one of the meditations that was helpful in your day-to-day life.

 Your awareness around something shifted.

 You learned something new about yourself.

 Your relationship to the Universe deepened.

 You developed more self-compassion or self-love.

 You witnessed one or more synchronicities since reading the book: you met the right people at the right time, were at the right place at the right time, or received some signs along the way.

⭐ You feel lighter than when you started reading the book or the opposite: the book has made you aware of how much more you need to release and you'll embark on a longer self-healing journey.

⭐ You are more able to live in the Now. You learned something new about yourself.

⭐ You are able to process your emotional landscape better. You developed more self-compassion or self-love.

⭐ You feel more gratitude in general, even for the little things.

⭐ Some relationships improved or the opposite: you were able to let go of people who were sucking up all your energy.

⭐ You might feel like you have more energy.

⭐ Maybe your health improved.

I haven't co-created my goal by the time I finished reading the book. Did I do something wrong?

Absolutely not. If you read through all the chapters and did all the meditations, including Step 11, The Art Of Letting Go, it's time to detach from your goal and to believe in divine timing. Some goals get co-created instantly, while others might take longer to materialise into your physical reality. You planted the seeds and now it's time to water them from time to time and watch the seeds grow. Some goals, of course, take longer to materialise than others, so depending on what you picked, you might have to practice patience for a while. And as I pointed out before: keep a weekly ritual of tuning in as to what else to work on while your co-creation desire is in the process of becoming a physical reality.

 I decided on a different co-creation goal in the middle of the book. Should I start from step 1 again or is it okay to keep going?

Definitely start from Step 1 again. Each step is geared towards that specific goal and missing out on the advice, healing and guidance from previous steps might mean that you won't have enough co-creation energy to materialise this new goal into your physical reality.

 I have a chronic illness I wish to heal from. Can this book help me?

Make sure you get medical advice and care first and foremost. Healing and meditation definitely have their place in a person's healing and recovery journey, but on their own, they might not be enough. While miracles exist, of course, I'm a strong advocate for alternative healing methods (which includes meditation and energy healing) working very well alongside conventional medicine.

 I can't decide between multiple important co-creation goals. Can you help?

The first step is to do the accompanying meditation "Pick

a co-creation goal" to gain more clarity. If that doesn't bring you further, choose the co-creation desire that is the most urgent one. Otherwise choose the goal which, once accomplished, feels best when you imagine it has already happened.

Tune into all your co-creation goals and visualise them. Which one feels most joyful or important to you while visualising? Pay attention to your body while visualising: maybe you feel a shiver, get goosebumps, your heart rate goes up, or you have a significant emotional response. Choose what makes you feel the most.

At the same time, be aware that once we start working on ourselves, even if only on one goal, oftentimes other things fall into place for other co-creation goals at the same time. The work you do might have ripple effects. So be open towards advancing other goals, even if you only focus on one goal during this book. Once you finish working on your first co-creation goal, you can start from scratch with your next one.

About The Author

Lais Stephan is a half Brazilian, half German writer, modern-day spiritual leader, Psychic Healer, and Women's Empowerment Coach. She assists women with increasing their co-creation and abundance energy by releasing traumatic memories from their bodies, minds and souls, and by teaching them how to tap into their own intuitive gifts so they can co-create the life they desire and deserve to live.

Lais has worked with thousands of women around the world through her intensive one-on-one programs and her online group courses.

You can follow her here:

 Laisstephan.com & Abundantchicks.com

 @Laisstephan_Author

 Facebook.com/LaisStephan

Acknowledgements

First of all, I would love to acknowledge my beloved Universe. I couldn't have written this book without you. We have come a long way together, haven't we? I'm in love with your humorous, light-hearted way of explaining things. Our conversations were my inspiration to write this book. Thank you, with all my heart, for always showing up and providing me with inspiration. Thank you for loving and guiding me on my path, even through all those times I wanted to give up and not publish any books.

Isa, my sweet Earth angel, you are the closest I have been to the Divine here on Earth. You continue to teach me the strongest lesson of all: the one about unconditional love. You are by far my favourite human being. Your pure heart, your innocence, your humour – all of that inspires me to become a better human being on a daily basis. My prayers are always the same: may you recover fully from your PTSD and shine your bright light again.

John, my love, without your nurturing, your daily delicious cooking and your help making sure I have a grounded routine, this work would never have been possible. You always believed in me and encouraged me to keep going even when I was close to giving up. Without you, this book wouldn't exist. Thank you from the bottom of my heart.

Mum, you have been tied up with Isa and her severe mental health crises year after year. I can only imagine how difficult it must have been and still is. I do feel your energetic support, though, so so deeply. I know

I could probably write gibberish and you would still love it. Thank you for believing in me, always. Thank you for incarnating as my mother, even when you sometimes tell me that I most likely tried to convince you for a long time to come "down here" again.

My next love note goes to every single woman I have had the honour to work with over the last decade. I want to say thank you for being the inspiration and foundation for this book and many more to follow. You are far too many to list here, but know that our encounter was special to me. Know that while I acted as a spiritual teacher or healer, you taught me so much in return. You continuously inspired me to grow, to do better, and to become who I am today. While my journey is nowhere finished, thank you to each and every one of you for having played a huge part in my spiritual development. I love you!

Pierre Billeter, you have been a constant source of spiritual wisdom in the most grounded way. You were my biggest supporting force while living in Geneva, giving me access to your magnificent "cabinet" where I taught many courses and welcomed in so many clients. Without your support, I would never have been able to enjoy work and start accumulating case studies for my books. Thank you from the bottom of my heart.

Nicole V., you just know how to make my life better, don't you? My life is beautiful and rich because you are in it. Thank you for being one of the most amazing souls I have had the honour to meet. You are my true soul sister and I love you more than I can even put into words.

Ivana, you have been a constant friend throughout my time writing this book, always listening to my ramblings about feeling stuck and motivating me to keep going. You are such a great listener and your support means the world to me. Thank you, I love you!

Alnaaze and Laura, oh my goodness, there will never be a writing group I will love more. There is something binding us together, keeping us together, motivating us to work on bigger projects and to think about the collective field we are here to serve. I deeply believe the Universe conspired to have us meet and is still guiding us. We have a big mission together and I can't wait to see what will come out of it. I love you to the moon and back!

Anne and Alexis, my sweet poet warriors, I am deeply grateful for having met you in Ubud, Bali, when I first started writing from the Universe's point of view. I miss our regular meetings at Yellow Flower, Lala & Lili and Warung Pulau Kelapa.

Having an idea and turning it into a book is as hard as it sounds. It's both challenging and rewarding at the same time. This book wouldn't exist without these special individuals who helped make this happen:

A huge thank you to Rosemary Sneeringer for editing and polishing this book and for believing in its success. It was an honour to work with you.

Laura Burge, my editing wizard: thank you for editing my introduction that I kept rewriting multiple times. It's a nice feeling to know you were involved with your editing magic in my book.

Ces Rosanna Price: you, like no other, understood my vision for this book. Your illustrations, the page design and the gorgeous cover filled my heart with immense gratitude. Without these, the book wouldn't be what it is. Thank you, thank you, thank you!

Loriana Valente, my music producer extraordinaire: without you, my meditations wouldn't have been as amazing as they are. Your background music, which you composed and produced specifically for this book, is beautiful. I'm looking forward to future projects with you. https://www.linktr.ee/lorianavalente

Thank you, Baba Omar (CEO of Fairtone Records / Artist Developer) for supporting my book by mastering the meditation sound. I was overjoyed when Loriana told me you would support us. Thank you from the bottom of my heart.

And last but not least, a huge thank you to every single reader. Having you read this book means the world to me. May your co-creation journey unfold beautifully

CPSIA information can be obtained
at www.ICGtesting.com
Printed in the USA
LVHW022022020821
694140LV00007B/193